www.markdg.com

Ordering Information:
Quantity sales. Special discounts are available on quantity purchases by corporations, associations, and others. For details, contact the publisher at the address above.

Printed in the United States of America
Publisher's Cataloging-in-Publication data

Gormley, Mark.
How To Look Smart / Mark Gormley

ISBN 978-1-387-00987-9

Dedicated to Jesus

Preface

Dear Reader,

With this vast, life-changing publication comes great responsibility. You now have THE secret weapon in creating a total false sense of intelligence. Congratulations on your new adventure.

Like you, I was once a dunce. I couldn't tell a Hefeweizen from a Guggenheimen, a Rza from the Gza, a David Letterman from Letter Davidman. I had it bad. The girls didn't like me. The boys didn't like me. The cats and dogs didn't even like me. That all changed the day I both discovered, and created, "How To Look Smart."

It was a cool summer day in February. I had just picked up my helicopter hat from the hat store when it hit me: a car. I went flying, and the hat spun me into a tree. I was stuck there for days. While in the tree, I made a friend: a talking squirrel. But he only spoke Portuguese! Luckily, I had a Portuguese friend. But he only spoke Portuguese too! I was out of luck. I left the talking squirrel in the tree and went back on my way to meet my girlfriend, Chrissy G.

Chrissy asked where I'd been the last few days. I told her about the talking squirrel and she rolled her eyes, as she usually does. "When are you going to make some real friends?"

That's when I found out something so big that I had to twirl my hat out of excitement. So huge that I'd need an entire book, maybe two, to detail it. So gigantic that I could sell it and finally quit my job at the jerk store. The other jerks and I had come up with the perfect plan. A book about camouflaging our idiocy. A book that would allow us to hide in plain sight with the boys of wall street. With the teachers and doctors. With the mailmen and scientists. And thus, my work began.

Six years and 37 chapters later, I have completed my masterpiece. And now I bestow it unto you. With this book, you'll no longer have to worry about fitting in with the best of 'em. You'll BE the best of 'em. Now YOU'RE the rock star who the chicks are gonna be staring at! Get used to it, fella. It's gonna be a wild ride. So get out there and look smart. People are watching!

Don't be afraid to email me with any questions or comments. Congratulations on your new look on life!

Sincerely,
Mark Gormley
Markdg.com@gmail.com

HOW TO LOOK SMART

Mark Gormley

Chapter 1

Look interested. Pretend there is useful information here.
Aim cover towards victim.

Look interested. Pretend there is useful information here.
Aim cover towards victim.

Look interested. Pretend there is useful information here.
Aim cover towards victim.

Look interested. Pretend there is useful information here.
Aim cover towards victim.

Chapter 2

Look interested. Pretend there is useful information here.
Aim cover towards victim.

Look interested. Pretend there is useful information here.
Aim cover towards victim.

Look interested. Pretend there is useful information here.
Aim cover towards victim.

Look interested. Pretend there is useful information here.
Aim cover towards victim.

Chapter 3

Look interested. Pretend there is useful information here.
Aim cover towards victim.

Look interested. Pretend there is useful information here.
Aim cover towards victim.

Look interested. Pretend there is useful information here.
Aim cover towards victim.

Look interested. Pretend there is useful information here.
Aim cover towards victim.

Chapter 4

Look interested. Pretend there is useful information here.
Aim cover towards victim.

Look interested. Pretend there is useful information here.
Aim cover towards victim.

Look interested. Pretend there is useful information here.
Aim cover towards victim.

Look interested. Pretend there is useful information here.
Aim cover towards victim.

Chapter 5

Look interested. Pretend there is useful information here.
Aim cover towards victim.

Look interested. Pretend there is useful information here.
Aim cover towards victim.

Look interested. Pretend there is useful information here.
Aim cover towards victim.

Look interested. Pretend there is useful information here.
Aim cover towards victim.

Chapter 6

Look interested. Pretend there is useful information here.
Aim cover towards victim.

Look interested. Pretend there is useful information here.
Aim cover towards victim.

Look interested. Pretend there is useful information here.
Aim cover towards victim.

Look interested. Pretend there is useful information here.
Aim cover towards victim.

Chapter 7

Look interested. Pretend there is useful information here.
Aim cover towards victim.

.

Look interested. Pretend there is useful information here.
Aim cover towards victim.

Look interested. Pretend there is useful information here.
Aim cover towards victim.

Look interested. Pretend there is useful information here.
Aim cover towards victim.

Chapter 8

Look interested. Pretend there is useful information here.
Aim cover towards victim.

Look interested. Pretend there is useful information here.
Aim cover towards victim.

Look interested. Pretend there is useful information here.
Aim cover towards victim.

Look interested. Pretend there is useful information here.
Aim cover towards victim.

Chapter 9

Look interested. Pretend there is useful information here.
Aim cover towards victim.

Look interested. Pretend there is useful information here.
Aim cover towards victim.

Look interested. Pretend there is useful information here.
Aim cover towards victim.

Look interested. Pretend there is useful information here.
Aim cover towards victim.

Chapter 10

Look interested. Pretend there is useful information here.
Aim cover towards victim.

Look interested. Pretend there is useful information here.
Aim cover towards victim.

Look interested. Pretend there is useful information here.
Aim cover towards victim.

Look interested. Pretend there is useful information here.
Aim cover towards victim.

Chapter 11

Look interested. Pretend there is useful information here.
Aim cover towards victim.

Look interested. Pretend there is useful information here.
Aim cover towards victim.

Look interested. Pretend there is useful information here.
Aim cover towards victim.

Look interested. Pretend there is useful information here.
Aim cover towards victim.

Chapter 12

Look interested. Pretend there is useful information here.
Aim cover towards victim.

Look interested. Pretend there is useful information here.
Aim cover towards victim.

Look interested. Pretend there is useful information here.
Aim cover towards victim.

Look interested. Pretend there is useful information here.
Aim cover towards victim.

Chapter 13

Look interested. Pretend there is useful information here.
Aim cover towards victim.

Look interested. Pretend there is useful information here.
Aim cover towards victim.

Look interested. Pretend there is useful information here.
Aim cover towards victim.

Look interested. Pretend there is useful information here.
Aim cover towards victim.

Chapter 14

Look interested. Pretend there is useful information here.
Aim cover towards victim.

Look interested. Pretend there is useful information here.
Aim cover towards victim.

Look interested. Pretend there is useful information here.
Aim cover towards victim.

Look interested. Pretend there is useful information here.
Aim cover towards victim.

Chapter 15

Look interested. Pretend there is useful information here.
Aim cover towards victim.

Look interested. Pretend there is useful information here.
Aim cover towards victim.

Look interested. Pretend there is useful information here.
Aim cover towards victim.

Look interested. Pretend there is useful information here.
Aim cover towards victim.

Chapter 16

Look interested. Pretend there is useful information here.
Aim cover towards victim.

Look interested. Pretend there is useful information here.
Aim cover towards victim.

Look interested. Pretend there is useful information here.
Aim cover towards victim.

Look interested. Pretend there is useful information here.
Aim cover towards victim.

Chapter 17

Look interested. Pretend there is useful information here.
Aim cover towards victim.

Look interested. Pretend there is useful information here.
Aim cover towards victim.

Look interested. Pretend there is useful information here.
Aim cover towards victim.

Look interested. Pretend there is useful information here.
Aim cover towards victim.

Chapter 18

Look interested. Pretend there is useful information here.
Aim cover towards victim.

Look interested. Pretend there is useful information here.
Aim cover towards victim.

Look interested. Pretend there is useful information here.
Aim cover towards victim.

Look interested. Pretend there is useful information here.
Aim cover towards victim.

Chapter 19

Look interested. Pretend there is useful information here.
Aim cover towards victim.

Look interested. Pretend there is useful information here.
Aim cover towards victim.

Look interested. Pretend there is useful information here.
Aim cover towards victim.

Look interested. Pretend there is useful information here.
Aim cover towards victim.

Chapter 20

Look interested. Pretend there is useful information here.
Aim cover towards victim.

Look interested. Pretend there is useful information here.
Aim cover towards victim.

Look interested. Pretend there is useful information here.
Aim cover towards victim.

Look interested. Pretend there is useful information here.
Aim cover towards victim.

Chapter 21

Look interested. Pretend there is useful information here.
Aim cover towards victim.

Look interested. Pretend there is useful information here.
Aim cover towards victim.

Look interested. Pretend there is useful information here.
Aim cover towards victim.

Look interested. Pretend there is useful information here.
Aim cover towards victim.

Chapter 22

Look interested. Pretend there is useful information here.
Aim cover towards victim.

Look interested. Pretend there is useful information here.
Aim cover towards victim.

Look interested. Pretend there is useful information here.
Aim cover towards victim.

Look interested. Pretend there is useful information here.
Aim cover towards victim.

Chapter 23

Look interested. Pretend there is useful information here.
Aim cover towards victim.

Look interested. Pretend there is useful information here.
Aim cover towards victim.

Look interested. Pretend there is useful information here.
Aim cover towards victim.

Look interested. Pretend there is useful information here.
Aim cover towards victim.

Chapter 24

Look interested. Pretend there is useful information here.
Aim cover towards victim.

Look interested. Pretend there is useful information here.
Aim cover towards victim.

Look interested. Pretend there is useful information here.
Aim cover towards victim.

Look interested. Pretend there is useful information here.
Aim cover towards victim.

Chapter 25

Look interested. Pretend there is useful information here.
Aim cover towards victim.

Look interested. Pretend there is useful information here.
Aim cover towards victim.

Look interested. Pretend there is useful information here.
Aim cover towards victim.

Look interested. Pretend there is useful information here.
Aim cover towards victim.

Chapter 26

Look interested. Pretend there is useful information here.
Aim cover towards victim.

Look interested. Pretend there is useful information here.
Aim cover towards victim.

Look interested. Pretend there is useful information here.
Aim cover towards victim.

Look interested. Pretend there is useful information here.
Aim cover towards victim.

Chapter 27

Look interested. Pretend there is useful information here.
Aim cover towards victim.

Look interested. Pretend there is useful information here.
Aim cover towards victim.

Look interested. Pretend there is useful information here.
Aim cover towards victim.

Look interested. Pretend there is useful information here.
Aim cover towards victim.

Chapter 28

Look interested. Pretend there is useful information here.
Aim cover towards victim.

Look interested. Pretend there is useful information here.
Aim cover towards victim.

Look interested. Pretend there is useful information here.
Aim cover towards victim.

Look interested. Pretend there is useful information here.
Aim cover towards victim.

Chapter 29

Look interested. Pretend there is useful information here.
Aim cover towards victim.

Look interested. Pretend there is useful information here.
Aim cover towards victim.

Look interested. Pretend there is useful information here.
Aim cover towards victim.

Look interested. Pretend there is useful information here.
Aim cover towards victim.

Chapter 30

Look interested. Pretend there is useful information here.
Aim cover towards victim.

Look interested. Pretend there is useful information here.
Aim cover towards victim.

Look interested. Pretend there is useful information here.
Aim cover towards victim.

Look interested. Pretend there is useful information here.
Aim cover towards victim.

Chapter 31

Look interested. Pretend there is useful information here.
Aim cover towards victim.

Look interested. Pretend there is useful information here.
Aim cover towards victim.

Look interested. Pretend there is useful information here.
Aim cover towards victim.

Look interested. Pretend there is useful information here.
Aim cover towards victim.

Chapter 32

Look interested. Pretend there is useful information here.
Aim cover towards victim.

Look interested. Pretend there is useful information here.
Aim cover towards victim.

Look interested. Pretend there is useful information here.
Aim cover towards victim.

Look interested. Pretend there is useful information here.
Aim cover towards victim.

Chapter 33

Look interested. Pretend there is useful information here.
Aim cover towards victim.

Look interested. Pretend there is useful information here.
Aim cover towards victim.

Look interested. Pretend there is useful information here.
Aim cover towards victim.

Look interested. Pretend there is useful information here.
Aim cover towards victim.

Chapter 34

Look interested. Pretend there is useful information here.
Aim cover towards victim.

Look interested. Pretend there is useful information here.
Aim cover towards victim.

Look interested. Pretend there is useful information here.
Aim cover towards victim.

Look interested. Pretend there is useful information here.
Aim cover towards victim.

Chapter 35

Look interested. Pretend there is useful information here.
Aim cover towards victim.

Look interested. Pretend there is useful information here.
Aim cover towards victim.

Look interested. Pretend there is useful information here.
Aim cover towards victim.

Look interested. Pretend there is useful information here.
Aim cover towards victim.

Chapter 36

Look interested. Pretend there is useful information here.
Aim cover towards victim.

Look interested. Pretend there is useful information here.
Aim cover towards victim.

Look interested. Pretend there is useful information here.
Aim cover towards victim.

Look interested. Pretend there is useful information here.
Aim cover towards victim.

Chapter 37

Look interested. Pretend there is useful information here.
Aim cover towards victim.

Look interested. Pretend there is useful information here.
Aim cover towards victim.

Look interested. Pretend there is useful information here.
Aim cover towards victim.

Look interested. Pretend there is useful information here.
Aim cover towards victim.

Look interested. Pretend there is useful information here.
Aim cover towards victim.

Look interested. Pretend there is useful information here.
Aim cover towards victim.

Look interested. Pretend there is useful information here.
Aim cover towards victim.

Look interested. Pretend there is useful information here.
Aim cover towards victim.

Look interested. Pretend there is useful information here.
Aim cover towards victim.

Look interested. Pretend there is useful information here.
Aim cover towards victim.

Look interested. Pretend there is useful information here.
Aim cover towards victim.

Look interested. Pretend there is useful information here.
Aim cover towards victim.

Look interested. Pretend there is useful information here.
Aim cover towards victim.

Look interested. Pretend there is useful information here.
Aim cover towards victim.

Look interested. Pretend there is useful information here.
Aim cover towards victim.

Look interested. Pretend there is useful information here.
Aim cover towards victim.

Look interested. Pretend there is useful information here.
Aim cover towards victim.

Look interested. Pretend there is useful information here.
Aim cover towards victim.

Look interested. Pretend there is useful information here.
Aim cover towards victim.

Look interested. Pretend there is useful information here.
Aim cover towards victim.

Look interested. Pretend there is useful information here.
Aim cover towards victim.

Look interested. Pretend there is useful information here.
Aim cover towards victim.

Look interested. Pretend there is useful information here.
Aim cover towards victim.

Look interested. Pretend there is useful information here.
Aim cover towards victim.

Look interested. Pretend there is useful information here. Aim cover towards victim.

Look interested. Pretend there is useful information here.
Aim cover towards victim.

Look interested. Pretend there is useful information here.
Aim cover towards victim.

Look interested. Pretend there is useful information here.
Aim cover towards victim.

Look interested. Pretend there is useful information here.
Aim cover towards victim.

Look interested. Pretend there is useful information here.
Aim cover towards victim.

Look interested. Pretend there is useful information here.
Aim cover towards victim.

Look interested. Pretend there is useful information here.
Aim cover towards victim.

Look interested. Pretend there is useful information here.
Aim cover towards victim.

Look interested. Pretend there is useful information here.
Aim cover towards victim.

Look interested. Pretend there is useful information here.
Aim cover towards victim.

Epilogue

I really hope you enjoyed the book. Don't forget that this can be used almost anywhere. Looking smart should now come with ease. A suggested approach is to read the book again and again until you have all of its contents memorized. An audio version is currently in the works so you can practice even while you're driving!

If you have any questions, feel free to email me. I have the answers to pretty much everything.

Your friend (and instructor),

Mark Gormley
Markdg.com@gmail.com

And that is how you take a joke too far.

Made in the USA
Las Vegas, NV
11 July 2021